Time Fragments

Traces of Newfoundand

The Artwork of
Margaret Ryall

number one in the

Komatik Press
Artists' Series

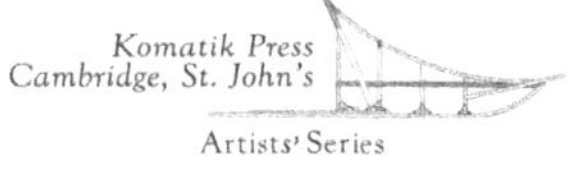

Published in Canada by

Komatik Press

62 Lower Street, Torbay, Newfoundland and Labrador,

A1K 1B3

www.komatikpress.com

rexkomatik@gmail.com

ISBN (paperback) 978-1-950065-02-8

ISBN (hardcover) 978-1-950065-04-2

ISBN (eBook) 978-1-950065-03-5

Book and cover design by Rex Passion

Artwork photographed by Ritche Perez 2020

Komatik Press Artists' Series

Introduction

In 2019, we created the Komatik Press *Artists' Series* to celebrate the visual artists of Newfoundland and Labrador, to explore the amazing diversity of their artistic practices, and to give artists an opportunity to talk about their work in their own words.

We are an experimental publisher using digital printing technology to discover areas that would not be open to traditional publishers due to cost. We use digital design, on-demand printing and distribution, and social media to reach a worldwide readership at a reasonable price with both print and e-books. We want to use this revolutionary technology to expose a large audience to a wide diversity of art and artists. We plan to examine a broad range of artistic forms: painting, sculpture, fiber art, photography, furniture, jewellery, street art and others; from many different groups of artists. For us at Komatik Press, this will be an exciting journey and we hope it will contribute to a wider appreciation for the grand diversity of art and artists in Newfoundland and Labrador. I am sure there will be some unexpected twists along the way.

Rex Passion
Komatik Press
Torbay, Newfoundland
2020

Time Fragments
Traces of Newfoundland

Margaret Ryall

Margaret Ryall's studio looks more like a cabinet shop than an artist's lair. There is a table saw and a chop saw and boxes of "special" wood pieces. As she says, the pieces find her, they jump out at her as she walks by. They are fragments of where she lives, fragments of Newfoundland's past.

In her loud, dusty workshop, she assembles these significant bits of local history into wooden bas-relief constructions worthy of Modernist architects.

R.P.

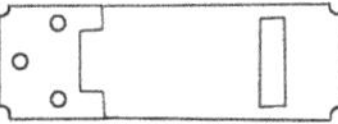

Artist's Statement

I find beauty in the ordinary and use a variety of media to draw attention to overlooked and discarded objects and materials. Collapsed buildings, peeling wallpaper, and broken objects are elevated in my mixed-media compositions and wood assemblages. I am interested in providing a second look, and I sometimes focus on layers and sometimes on abstract compositions to create new meaning.

In *Time Fragments* I explore a more minimal, reductive aesthetic where considerations of texture, colour, materiality, and structure dominate. This process of selection is akin to writing a haiku poem where every choice counts. The elimination of the unnecessary produces works of intimate scale that are sparse, focused, and poetic; they are as much about what isn't there as what is.

As my work becomes more structural, I recognize that my lifelong interest in architecture and design affects the forms I create. I must admit that I am an architect at heart.

Margaret M. Ryall
Duntara, Newfoundland
2019

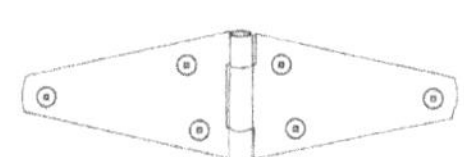

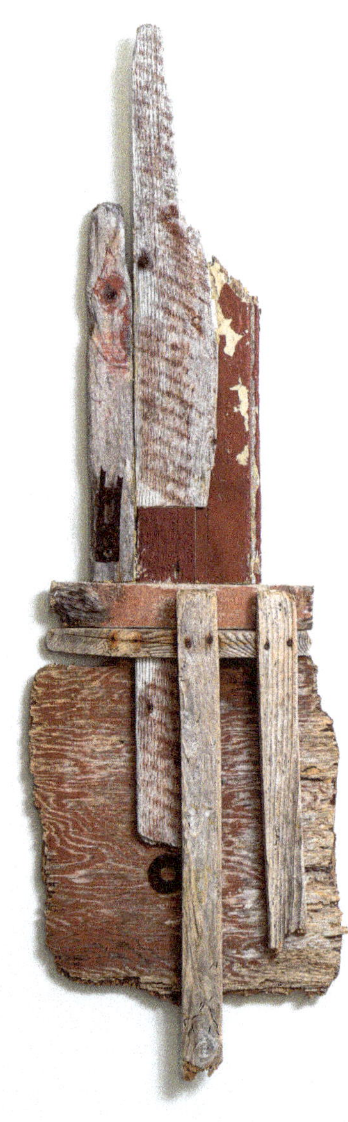

trap # 1

The colour red is consistently used to paint sheds on the Bonavista Peninsula. The curved piece of the lobster trap references fishing sheds in particular.

This piece moved my work in a new direction where editing became a very important part of the process until I was left with just enough to create a pleasing composition.

Shed and *Trap # 1* are larger and more complicated than my later works and both use pieces of lobster traps I found washed up on various beaches. There is little plastic trash on Newfoundland beaches, but plenty of broken wooden bits.

As the long vertical piece of wood was precarious, I tied it in using the tip of the hinge. I still have to be careful when handling it, but if it should break off, I will accept it as part of ongoing change as time passes.

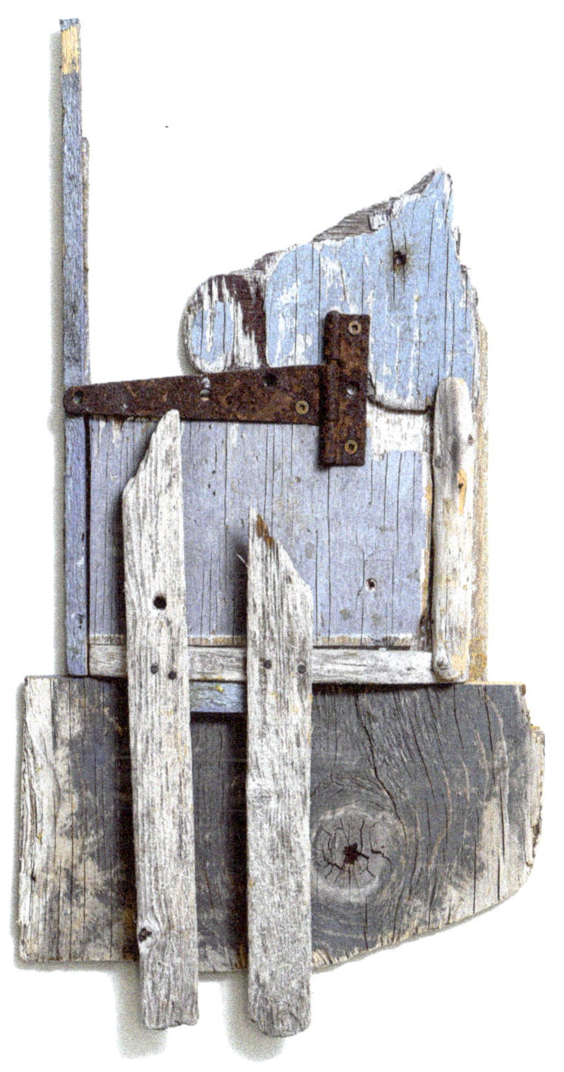

shed

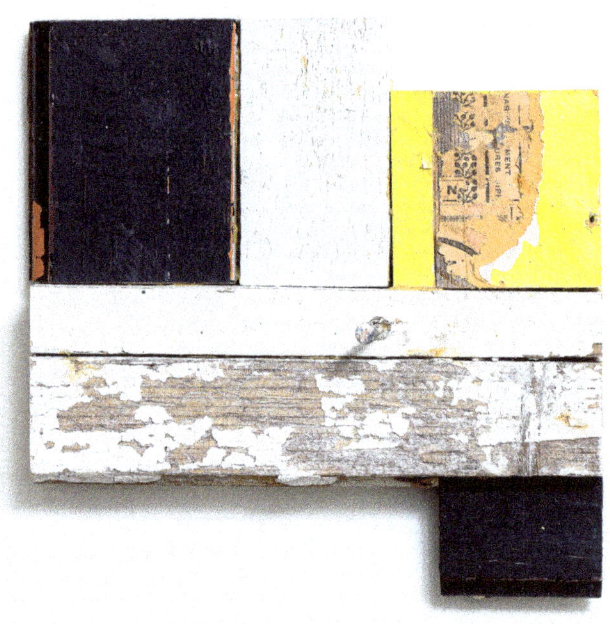

news

This is one of the first works where I was consistently thinking about straightforward compositions. I like the proportions and the simplicity. The lone nail acts as an avenue into the piece.

The bit of newspaper on the right adds interest to balance the rest of the composition while also suggesting lives lived in an old home.

It is a joy when I find wood with old newsprint underneath wallpaper. Sometimes it is about what the print says, but more often it is a contextual design element that indicates people's presence.

There is always history in the elements I choose for a construction. I am preserving that history, even if I don't know what it is. I try to take something old and make it new again and raise common materials to a higher level.

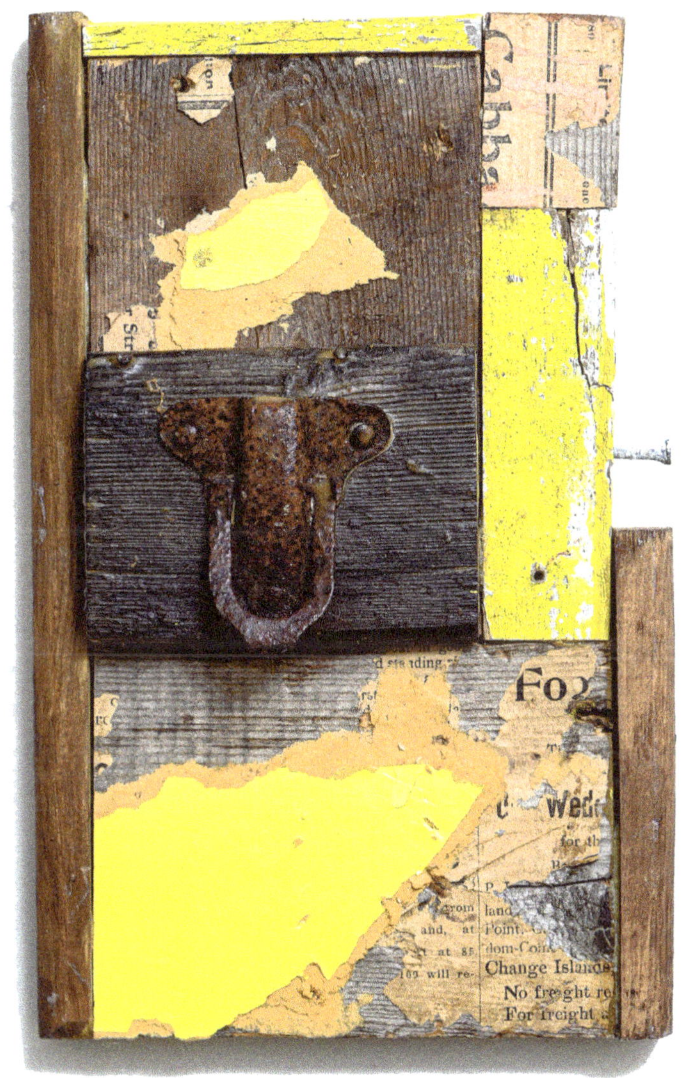

trunk

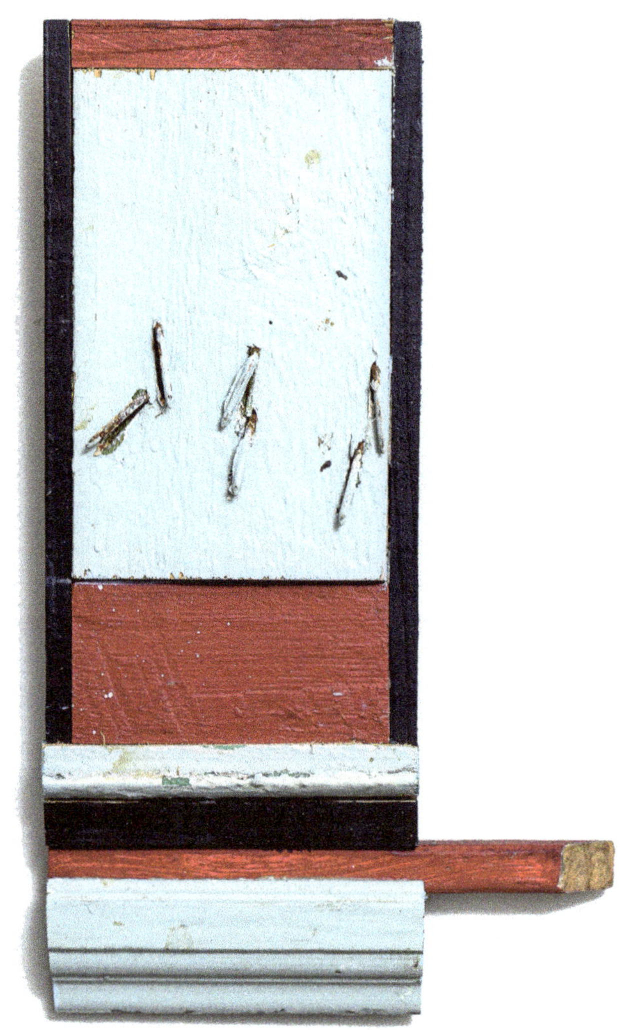

nails #2

I have big plastic trays in my studio where I keep all my cut-off pieces, sorted by colour. Searching through them is a favourite part of my process. Colours can come together in unexpected combinations when you lay them alongside one another. I have another tray called "specials." The blue piece with the nails was in the specials tray, and was the starting point for this work.

Because most of this composition is very contained, I wanted to add an avenue into it with the red strip.

The long orange board was the first piece chosen in this work. The latch made me wonder what was kept behind the door, what needed to be protected or secured. Was it something precious? The ragged top and broken bottom make me think that it was forcefully removed when the shed was torn down or fixed up.

I see the light blue, bamboo-like piece as quite special. A friend found it on the beach, and saved it for me. It's not really bamboo, but a wood moulding made to look like it.

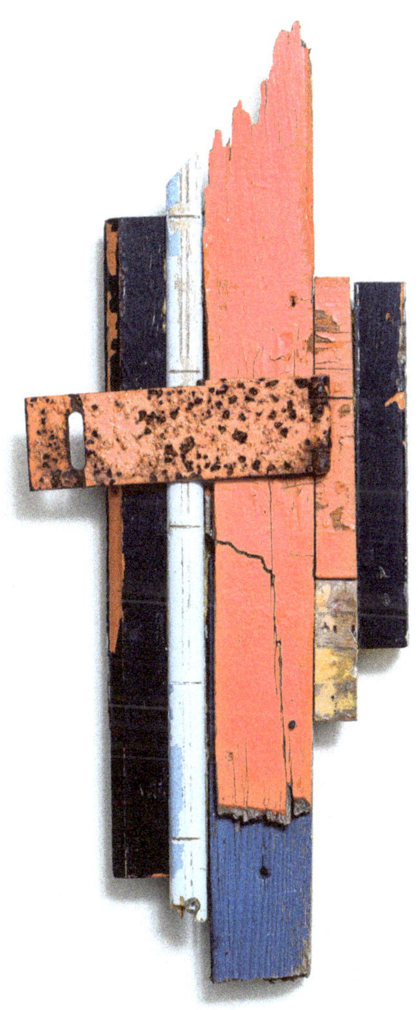

bamboo

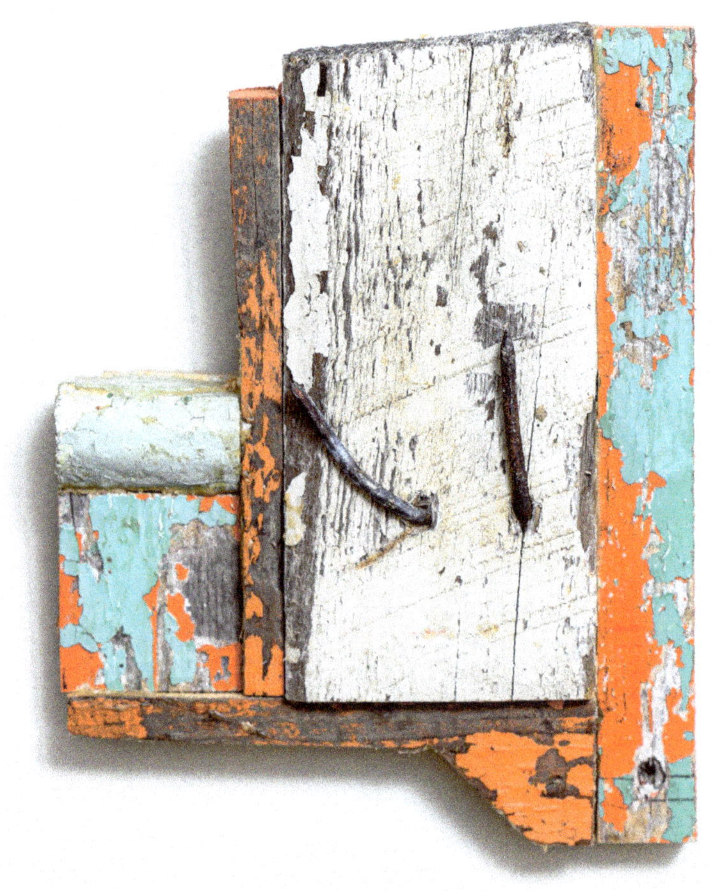

nailed

All of the wood for *Nailed* was found behind my Uncle Bill's house in Duntara. While he is no longer there, the house still is, and this wood is a testament to the various repairs he made over time. This is one of the rawest, roughest pieces in the series, and I really didn't like it much as I constructed it.

I love the contrast between the presence of the nails pounded in and bent over and the absence of the nail in the bottom right. There is a balance in the gentle curve at the top, the curved saw marks on the white piece and the rounded edges on the piece on the top left. There is nothing elegant about *Nailed*, but it is one of my favourites.

I had the blue pieces in my specials tray for quite a while, and the red cross came later. I couldn't seem to come up with a composition that was worthy of them but when they ended up on my work table, they had such energy together, a new work was born.

In order to make the composition work, I had to trim the cross a little, and find another red piece to add to the right to stop the horizontal flow of the blue. The small moulding at the bottom left and the reds are newer wood, so there is an old/new balance. The pencil marks are intriguing, but I don't know anything about them.

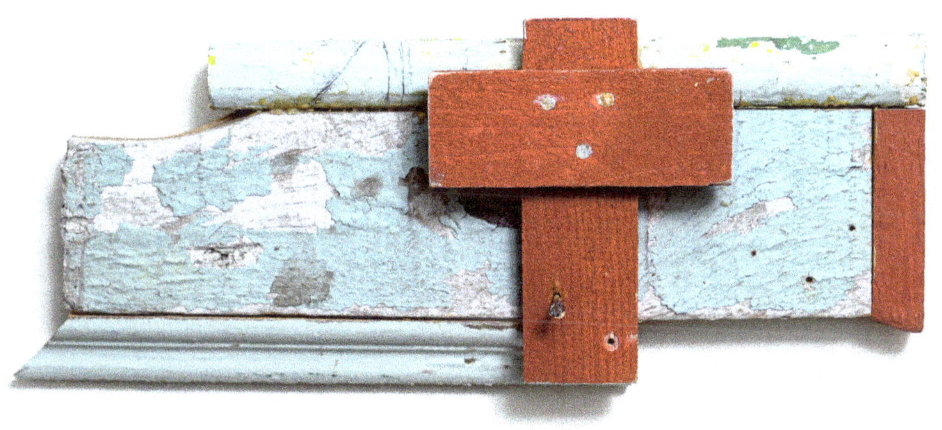

red cross

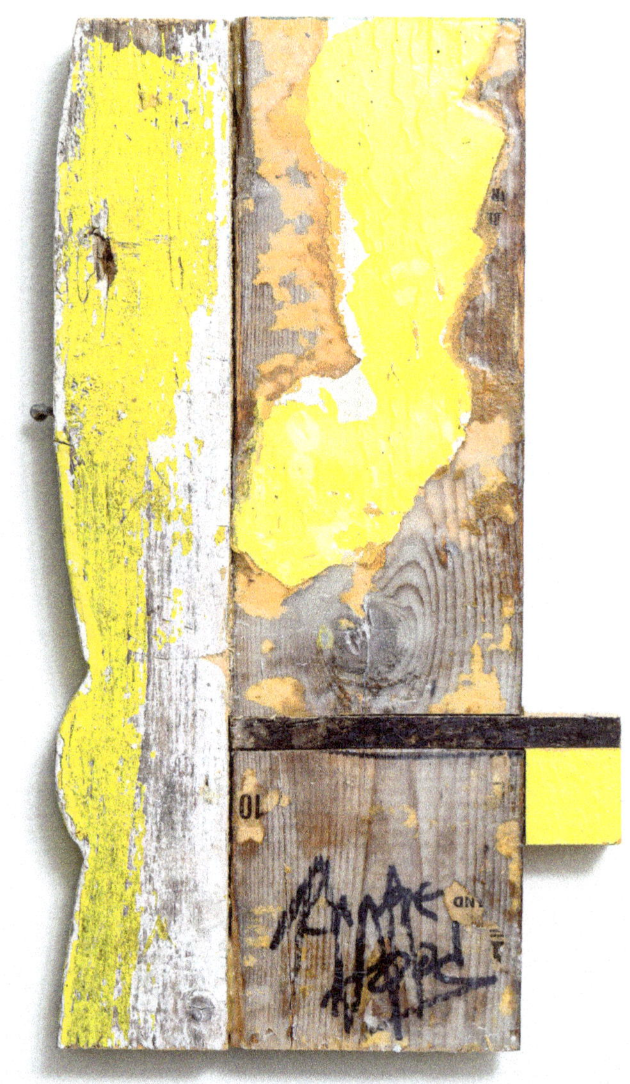

range hood

I am always excited when I find wood that has text on it, and hand-written text is even more exciting. Someone was obviously renovating a kitchen and planning things out on the wall. It looks as if there was some indecision in the process.

The contrast of yellow and black has a contemporary feel that could be the colours of a new, modern kitchen. The black strip is like a punctuation mark. It is between the top and the bottom in a proportion that felt right. One eigth of an inch either way would not have worked.

The idea of renovation caused me to make changes in the direction of my work.

The board marked "stove top" is from the same house as the one in *Range Hood*, and part of the same renovation. The plastic handle of the paint brush also suggests new beginnings.

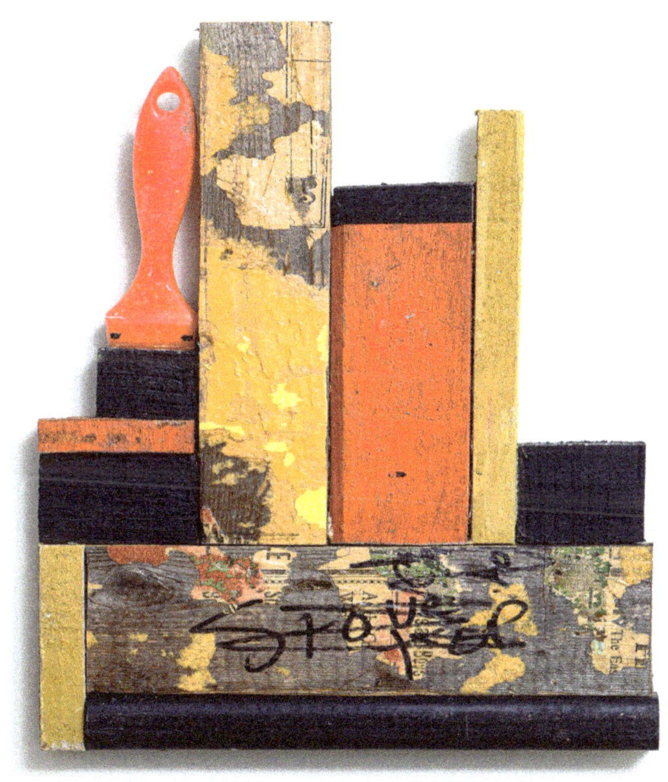

stove top

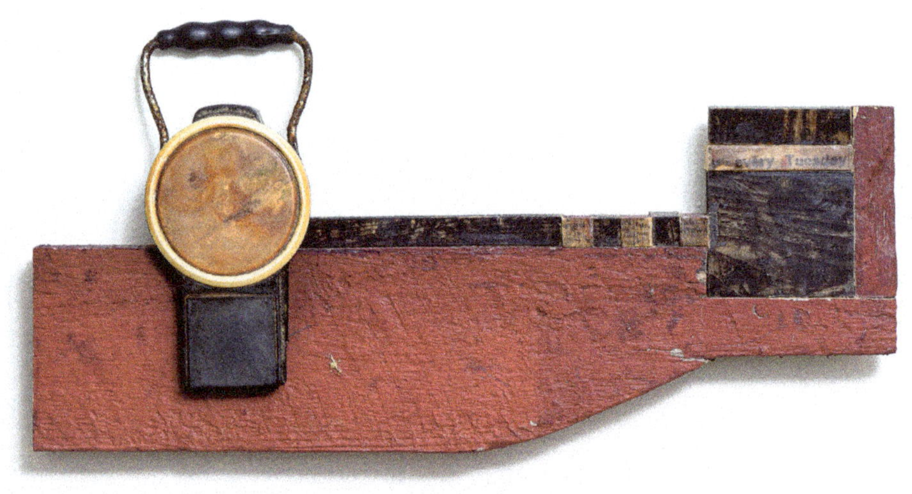

scale

The round piece with the handle is a scale, probably for weighing fish. It was a gift from my sister in Placentia and is the only piece in this series not from the Bonavista Peninsula. Some of the found text is obscure, but "every Tuesday" is distinct. I chose this bit of print to give the work a time reference. The dial is also obscured, so it might be taken for a clock. The red board is a piece from my neighbour's lawn chair which was beyond repair.

There were a lot of things swirling around in my mind when I began *Scale*: time, order, weight, and balance. It is one of my favourites.

Grid is one of only a few works where the major element is neither wood nor metal; the grid is plastic or fiberglass. Every piece is old except the black and white bits. I used wax to preserve the newspaper showing at the bottom.

I really thought I was going in a certain direction with this piece, but I just never found it. I like the balance between the elements: wood and plastic, old and new, and the open space behind the upper grid. It is more contained than many of the works in this series.

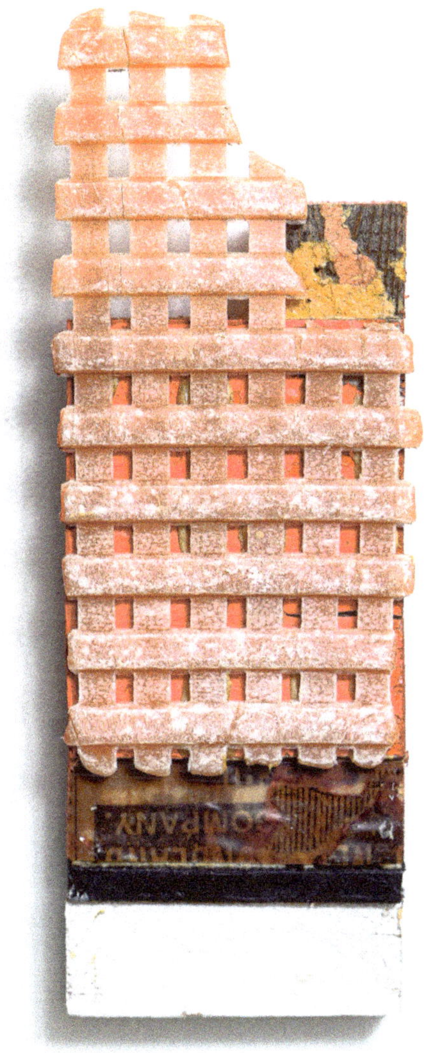

grid

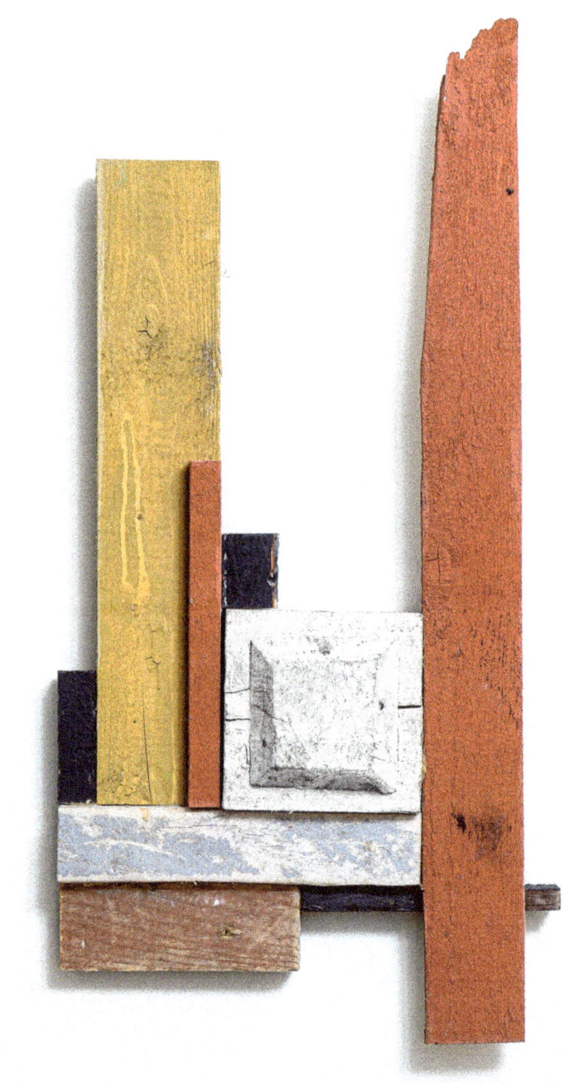

post cap

The three-dimensional post cap was a starting point for this work, which is all about directionality. With the pieces shooting out from the center, it is almost like it is rotating.

The longer pieces are open and free, while the others are confined and closed. The white post cap at the center is especially bound by the two longer pieces.

I added black at the last moment to balance the dominant, long, colourful elements, and bring attention to the center. It did not look finished without the black.

When I found this white board, I was attracted to the oval cutout for an electrical box because of its negative space, and the hint of the possibilities which electricity brought to rural life. Glimpses of faraway places gleaned from radio and television were woven into people's everyday experiences.

The black horizontal strip divides the work into old below and new above, with the vertical strip extending into space, hinting at communication towers and possibilities yet unheard of.

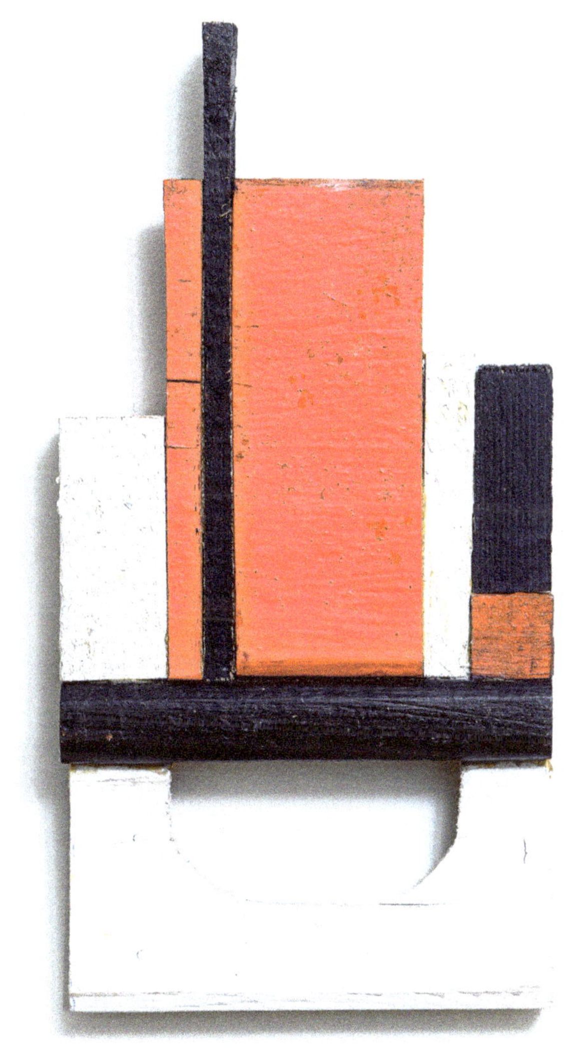

ceiling

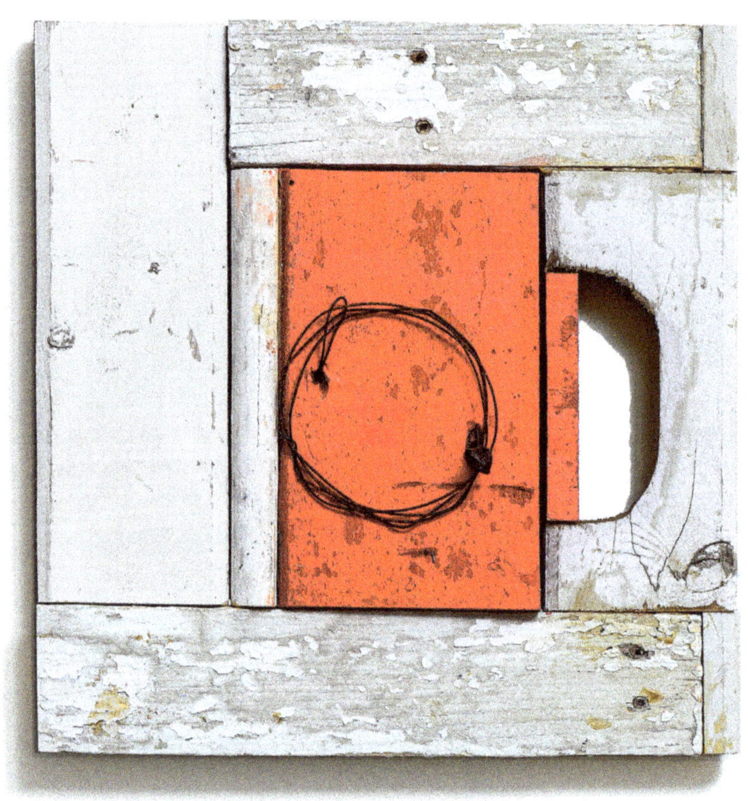

wired

Wired is the sister piece to *Ceiling*; the cut out in the white wood completes the circle for the electrical box. This work looks back in time to before the advent of electricity in rural Newfoundland.

The composition is bound on all sides and focuses our attention inward toward the heart of its energy. The nails and wire help to establish the time period.

A friend gave me several pieces of wood that obviously came from a very old trunk. After saving them for three years, I chose them for this composition. Trunks bring up thoughts of storage and travel, what you carry with you, and where you might go.

Lock is one of only a few horizontal works in this series. The suggestion of a cityscape hints that the travellers may be visiting a foreign capital. Other possibilities also exist in the yellow and red parallel lines.

I painted wax on the paper in an attempt to stop the passage of time.

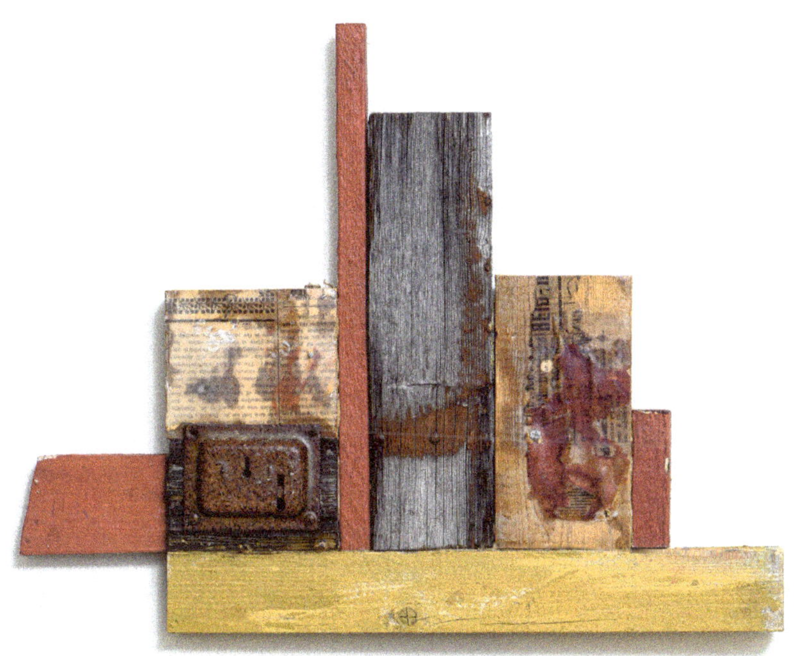

lock

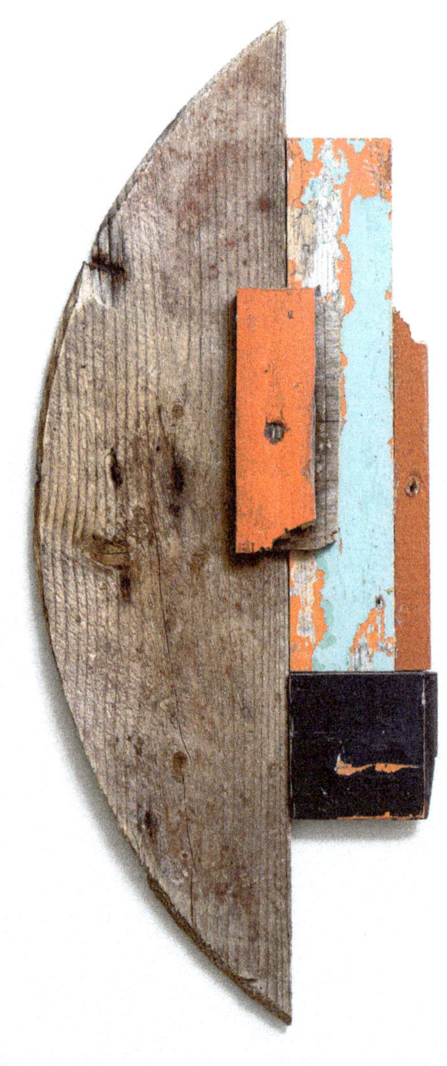

barrel with black square

It is never my intention to make my work resemble anything else; it is abstract art. When I accidentally turned this work on its side, it looked like a toy boat, which I did not find at all pleasing.

This barrel head, found in Keels, is the largest expanse of raw wood in any of my works. The orange piece of wood in the center can be turned slightly. This is intentional, so one can slightly alter the look, but only slightly as I do not want to give up too much control.

I find the nail holes in the red piece on the right and in the piece from Uncle Bill's house (*Nailed*) to be the absence of things; they are very attractive.

In my work, I definitely like celebrating common objects, such as the hinge that is the pivotal element in this work. The house-like enclosure elevates the ordinary hinge, which has seen its best days, to a higher level. Perhaps it is sitting on a window ledge where all can see it, or maybe I have constructed a kind of temple in its honour. The hinge is presented on a background of weathered plywood; the base is the curved part of a lobster pot.

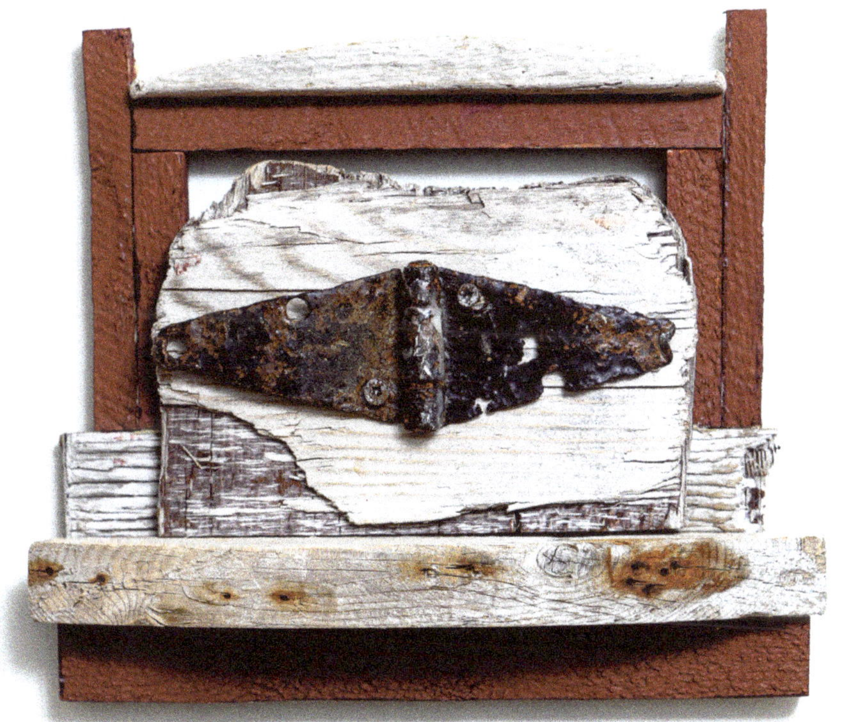

hinge

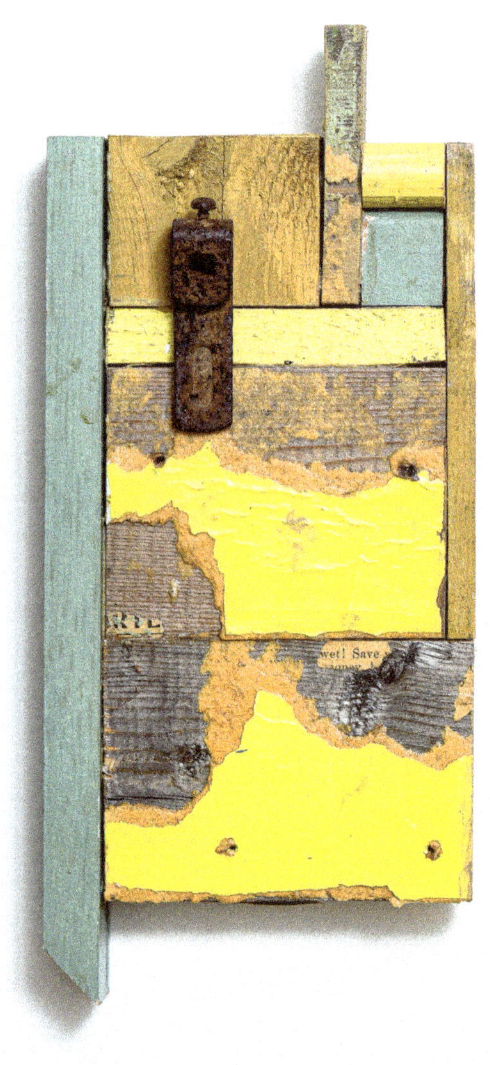

latch

There is something bright and cheery in the yellow in *Latch.* The green is new wood — some left over pieces from countertop edging — and its smoothness, contrasted against the rough, is pleasing. I also like the rhythm of the yellow wallpaper pieces. I always coat the wallpaper with wax or acrylic medium to prevent it from drying out. The small, rusty latch adds a contrasting colour and texture and an interesting form.

"wet! Save" just below the middle yellow is precious. I don't know what it means.

It is unusual for me to deviate from the parallel, but in Small Barrel the two elements on the right seem to wander apart at the top and diverge from the formal straight lines on the left.

In this work, elements that are from outside the house are paired with those from inside. The red pieces are parts of interior trim that have been left outside, and the paint has weathered and chipped; the oak barrel top is an outside element, something that might be found in a shed; the yellow is wallpaper.

I added the small squares to the gently curved right-hand edge, between the existing screws, to impart an almost musical rhythm.

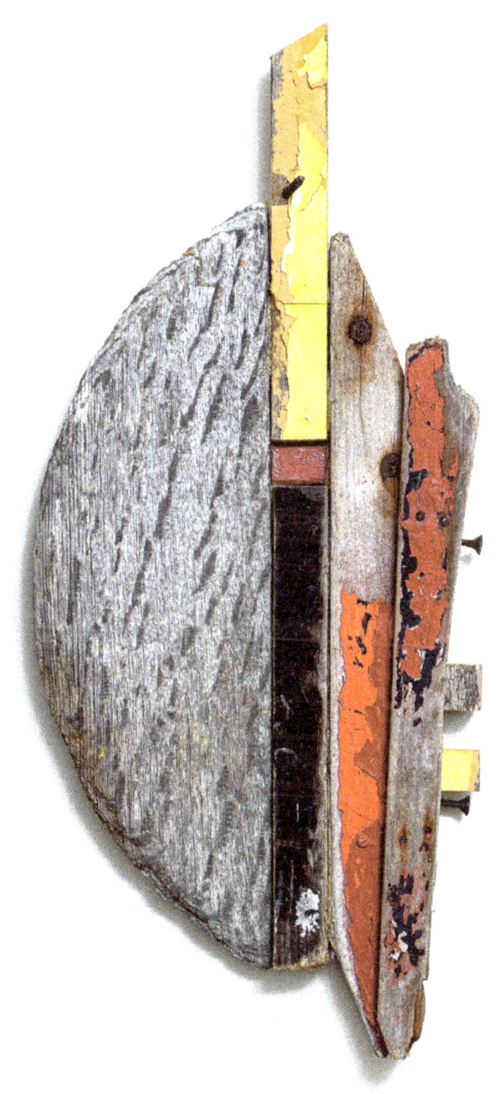

small barrel

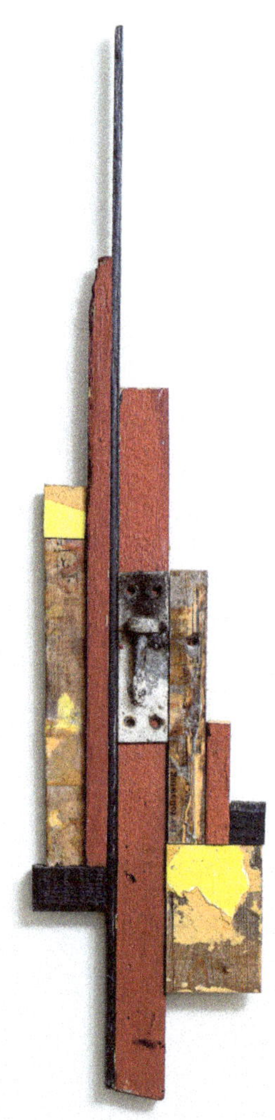

bolt

Bolt was done at the same time as the two barrel tops and *Scale*. It is the most soaring of my several vertical works. It is a skyscraper of a work, like the New York buildings that so moved me when I first saw them. I used black to anchor the downward movement of the soaring pieces.

When I was a teenager, I read about the Modernist architects; Frank Lloyd Wright and Frank Gehry are two of my favourites. I would not say that I was consciously influenced by their designs, but it is hard to deny their importance to my work.

In the small text opposite the bolt is "Department of Public Works" which was where my grandfather worked on the base at Argentia; a wonderful accidental discovery.

Unlike nearly all of my works in *Time Fragments*, *Wall* is totally enclosed. I like the different ways the black border restrains and exposes. The red and black are both confining, but the black more so.

When I am really stuck, I use black as a focus to restore balance. The yellow and black are also a very contemporary pairing.

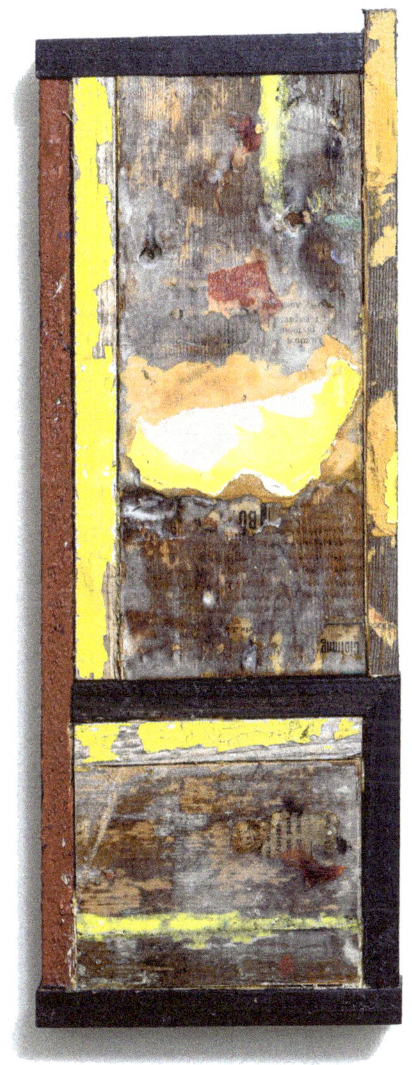

wall

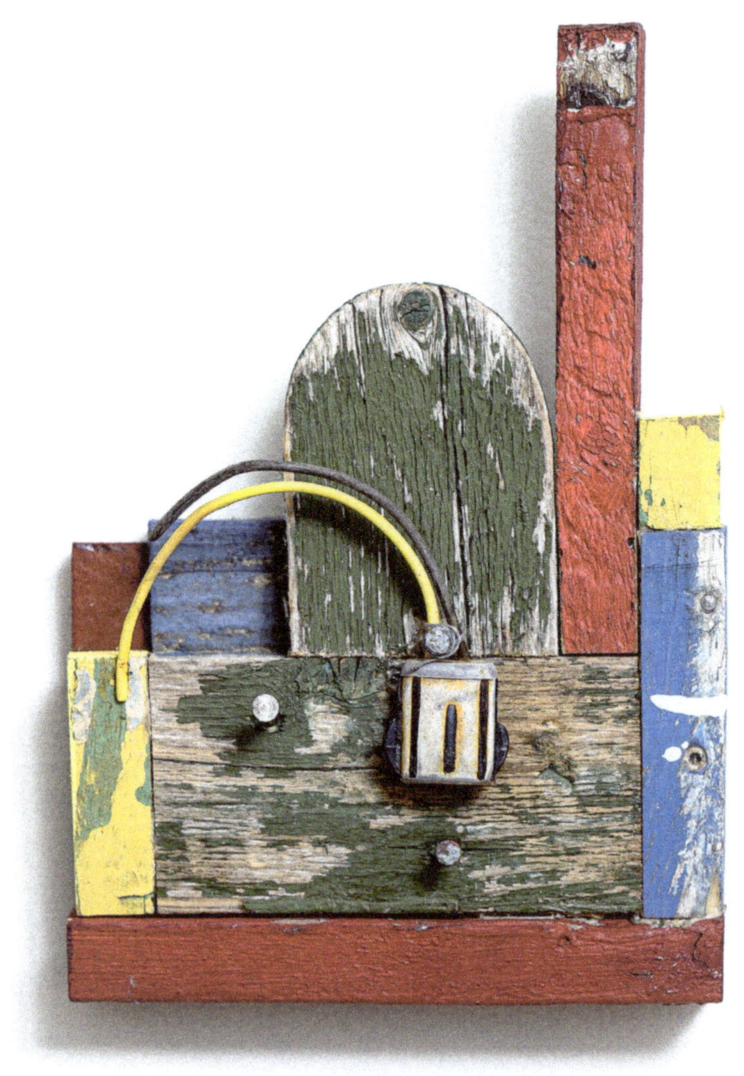

switch

Someone gave me a long, green fence paling, but I could never make it work. When I cut it down and added primary colours, it began to come together. I found the electrical bit when walking on the beach at Keels, and that set it apart.

Of my artistic criteria, balance is the most important and it can take a good deal of time to adjust the pieces until I get the balance just right.

Some of my works have been referred to as quirky. I can assure you that this adjective does not apply, usually. I find beauty in common, everyday objects, and I enhance their beauty with my constructions, perhaps sometimes in a quirky manner.

Although some view *Shelf* as awkward, it is the precarious nature of the composition that attracts me. The partially dislodged nails add to its unsettled feeling. The vertical blue strip was included as an effort to stabilize the base, but this strength is negated by the small pieces along the top suggesting homes that may be in peril.

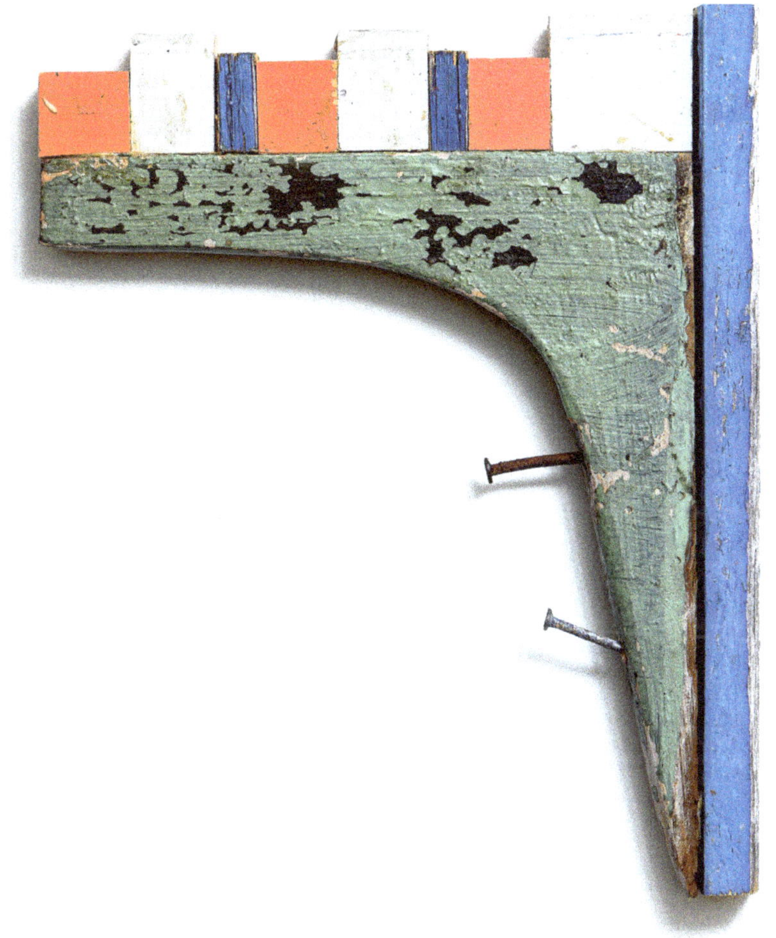

shelf

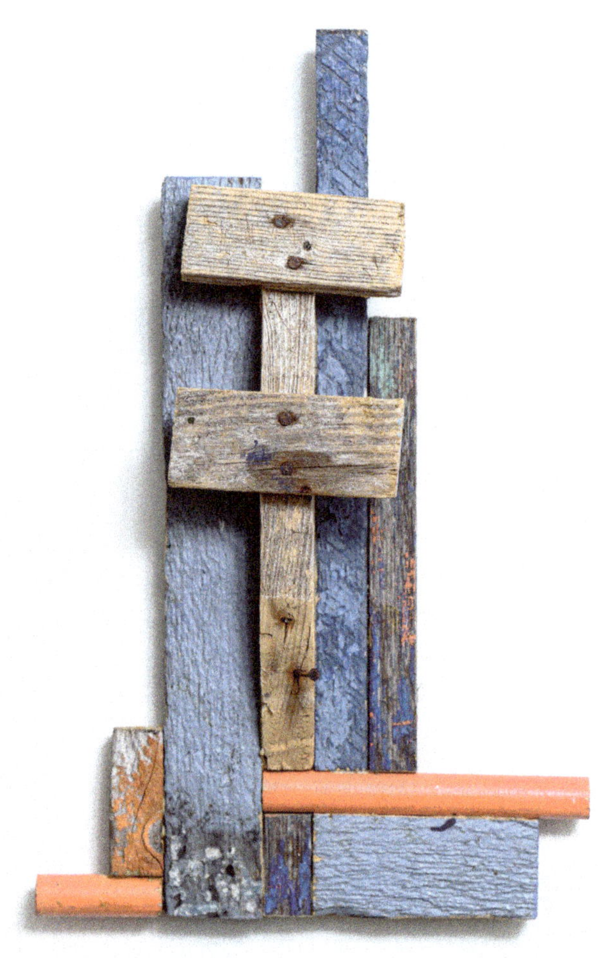

trap #2

All of the wood in *Trap # 2* was found in Duntara. There is a lively mix of old and new, as well as references to structures, furniture, and fishing equipment.

While the orange spindle is refined, and obviously well cared for, the remaining materials are aged, and marked by the passage of time and the ravages of weather.

I like the protrusion of the lobster trap and its less than perfect structure against the perfect form and surface of the spindle.

I find the simplicity of *Spindle* rather bold and powerful.

One of the two beige text pieces is totally enclosed, and one is open on two sides; it is the balance between these two that is critical.

The dowel is part of a rocker that blew off our porch in Duntara and broke. It balances old and new, blue and orange, smooth and rough all at the same time.

I have been told that I was channelling a famous Modernist architect when I chose the angled piece, but I am not sure.

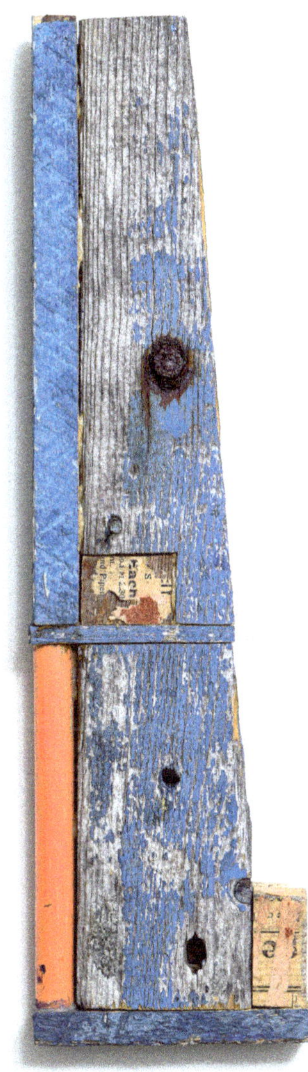

spindle

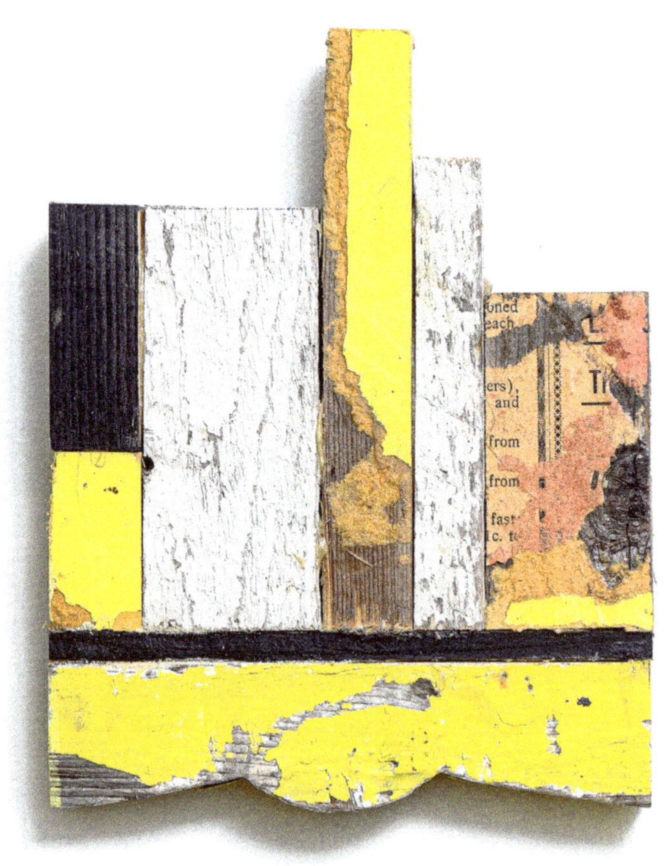

ledge

The sunny nature of these yellows always calls to me. The scalloped piece at the bottom was probably used underneath a window or shelf. While decorative, it also adds a certain amount of stability and a bit of whimsy. Imagine how different this composition would look if the bottom edge were straight. The strong horizontal line above the curved edge acts to hold the weight of the composition and to underline the commanding newspaper remnant on the right, with its suggestion of places and people but no specific news.

This work is number three in what I think of as my renovation works because of the directions written with a marker on the wood. The scalloped edge provides a counterbalance to the boldness of the black and of the wood grain. I have always wondered what directions the text in the upper right are giving to the builder.

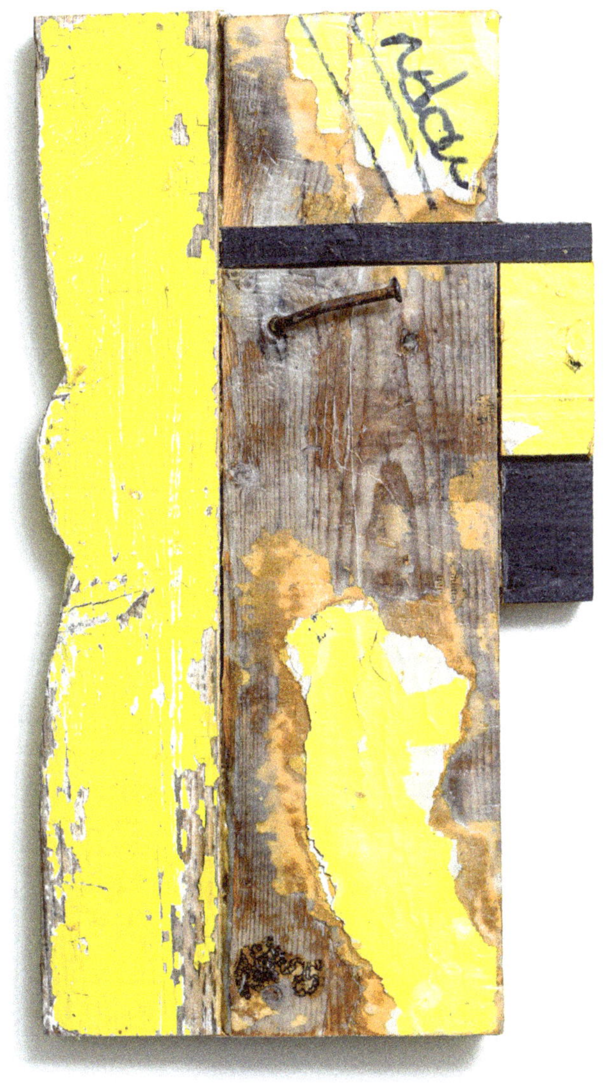

scalloped

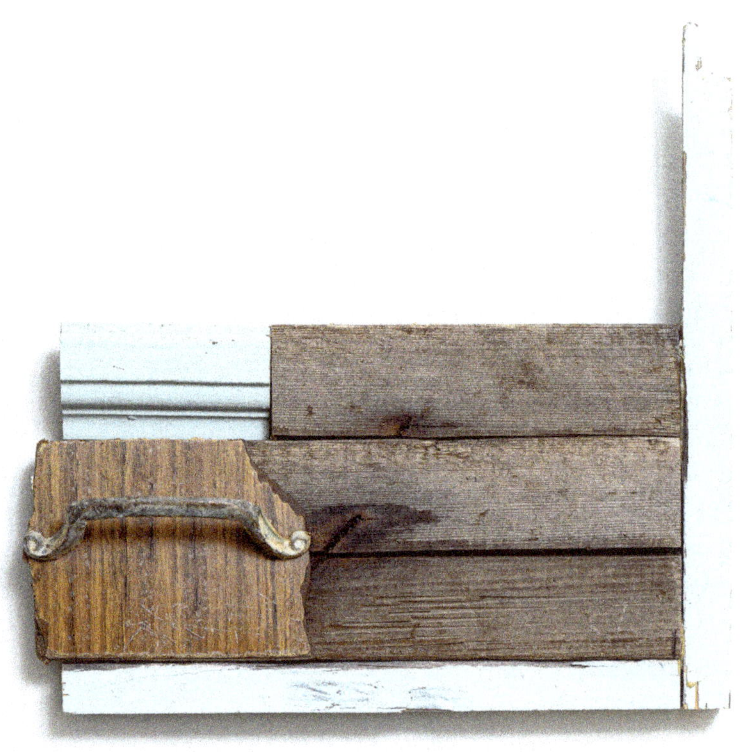

drawer

Serendipity is an important part of my practice. I was quite attracted to this drawer handle when I saw it.You could say it choose me. It became the centerpiece of *Drawer*. The drawer face is melamine, a kind of plastic, and that was attractive, too, when placed next to the raw wood.

I like the balance of the delicate blue with the rugged, raw, outside wood.

Trap #1

37 x 11 x 1¾ inches

94 x 27.9 x 4.4 cm

found objects

2018

Shed

23 x 12 x 2½ inches

58.4 x 30.5 x 6.4 cm

found objects

2018

News

8½ x 8 x 2 inches

21.6 x 20.3 x 5.1 cm

found objects

2018

Nails #2

12½ x 7½ x ¾ inches

31.8 x 19 x 1.9 cm

found objects

2018

Trunk

9¼ x 6 x 2 inches

23.5 x 15.2 x 5.1 cm

found objects

2018

Nails #2

12½ x 7½ x ¾ inches

31.8 x 19 x 1.9 cm

found objects

2018

Bamboo

19 x 8 x 2½ inches

48.3 x 20.3 x 6.4 cm

found objects

2018

Nailed

7 x 6 x 2½ inches

17.9 x 15.2 x 6.4 cm

found objects

2018

Red Cross

12 x 5 x 2½ inches

30.5 x 12.7 x 6.4 cm

found objects

2018

Range Hood

12 x 8 x 2½ inches

30.5 x 20.3 x 6.4 cm

found objects

2018

Stove Top

13 x 8 x 1½ inches

33 x 20.3 x 3.8 cm

found objects

2018

Scale

8 x 15½ x 2½ inches

20.3 x 39.4 x 6.4 cm

found objects

2018

Grid

10½ x 3¾ x 2½ inches

26.7 x 9.5 x 6.4 cm

found objects

2018

Post Cap

18 x 9 x 2½ inches

45.7 x 22.9 x 6.4 cm

found objects

2018

Ceiling

18 x 6 x 1¼ inches

45.7 x 15.2 x 3.2 cm

found objects

2018

Wired

11¼ x 11¼ x 1½ inches

28.6 x 28.6 x 3.8 cm

found objects

2018

Lock

16 x 12½ x 1½ inches

40.6 x 31.8 x 3.8 cm

found objects

2018

Barrel with Black Square

20 x 8½ x 1½ inches

50.8 x 21.6 x 3.8 cm

found objects

2017

Hinge

9¼ x 11 x 2¼ inches

23.5 x 27.9 x 5.7 cm

found objects

2019

Latch

13 x 5½ x 1¼ inches

33 x 14 x 3.2 cm

found objects

2018

Small Barrel

16 x 7 x 2 inches

40.6 x 17.9 x 5.1 cm

found objects

2018

Bolt

29 x 6 x 3½ inches

73.7 x 15.2 x 8.9 cm

found objects

2018

Wall

13½ x 5 x ¾ inches

34.3 x 12.7 x 1.9cm

found objects

2018

Switch

9½ x 6½ x 2½ inches

24.1 x 16.5 x 6.4 cm

found objects

2019

Shelf

10 x 8¼ x 1¾ inches

25.4 x 21 x 4.4 cm

found objects

2018

Trap #2

13 x 8½ x 2¾ inches

33 x 21.6 x 7 cm

found objects

2019

Spindle

15 x 4¼ x 1¾ inches

38.1 x 10.8 x 4.4 cm

found objects

2019

Ledge

8¼ x 6½ x ¾ inches

21 x 16.5 x 1.9 cm

found objects

2018

Scalloped

9¼ x 6 x 2 inches

23.5 x 15.2 x 5.1 cm

found objects

2018

Drawer

10 x 10½ x 2 inches

25.4 x 26.7 x 5.1 cm

found objects

2018

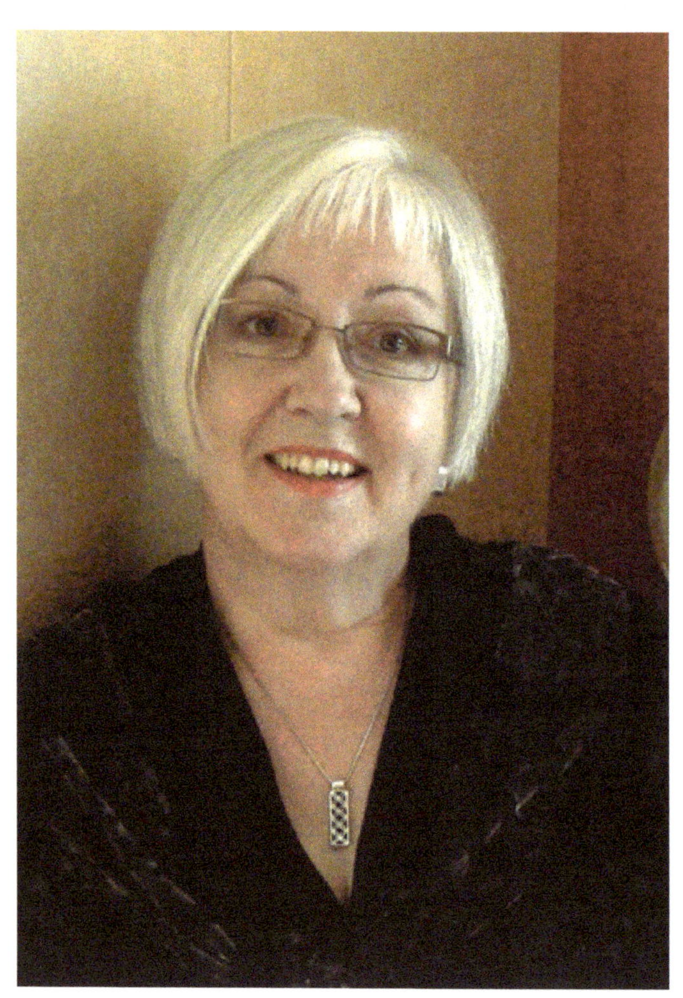

Margaret Ryall is a full-time artist who divides her time between her studio in St. John's and her workshop overlooking the harbour in Duntara, Newfoundland. She grew up in Placentia, where her parents encouraged her artistic endeavours from a young age. As an avid reader, books introduced her to cities, museums, and famous buildings around the world, and exposed her to a variety of art forms. Her later travels allowed her to observe many of these things first-hand.

After a fulfilling career as a teacher, Margaret shifted her focus to visual art and interior design. Her earliest paintings were garden themed; later work paired images of floral wallpaper with found objects using painting, collage, and mixed media. Her most recent assemblages, using discarded objects and ordinary materials, encourage viewers to look more deeply into forgotten fragments of the past. Her lifelong appreciation for architecture influences her abstract designs.

Margaret has participated in over seventy group and solo exhibitions of her work, which is in both public and private collections. She is represented by The Leyton Gallery of Fine Art in St. John's, Newfoundland.

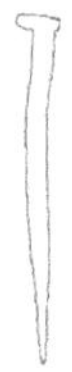

www.ingramcontent.com/pod-product-compliance
Ingram Content Group UK Ltd.
Pitfield, Milton Keynes, MK11 3LW, UK
UKHW061949290726
14090UKWH00021B/1151

9 781950 065028